YOU ARE BEAUTIFUL!

YOU ARE BEAUTIFUL!

53 Easy Ways To
Love Your Imperfect Self

Ana Wilde

Contents

LOVE
YOURSELF

"You Are Beautiful! 53 Easy Ways To Love Your Imperfect Self" is the ultimate guide to feeling good about how you look, so good that the world just has to agree you're someone to admire.

It's well known that when you're happy in your own skin, you give out positive signals about yourself that others pick up on, and this makes you a hundred times more attractive than those with little confidence or self-esteem.

There are many aspects to confidence, but this book focuses on the one that seems to affect women everywhere - how we feel about our appearance.

You might think you need to look fantastic to feel confident. But that's not the case.

In many ways, it really doesn't matter how you look.

An ordinary-looking woman with self-confidence lets her personality shine through, and this is much more captivating than the beauty who is unsure of herself and lets it show.

Although it has a positive effect on your confidence if you look your best, most of your self-esteem comes from within. It's too easy to imagine that you will only be happy when you change how you look, when what really matters is changing how you think about yourself.

We are all born feeling happy with ourselves, but as we grow up, it's too easy to feel we fall short of some arbitrary, impossible standard we believe we need to meet. Unkind words from adults and other kids give us the idea that we are somehow lacking in the looks department. And then we are constantly bombarded with the idea of perfection, not just from the thousands of media images we see every day, but also from our peers talking about how they fall short of the ideal, and we decide that, if they think they fall short, then we do too.

Enough already.

We're going to take this one step at a time so that you can feel fantastic about yourself no matter what is going on in the warped media world that is affecting you and your friends. You can feel on top of the world no matter what your starting point. It may not happen overnight because your feelings about yourself were not created in just one day, but by reading this book and implementing the strategies within it, you will quickly see changes for the better.

By using the ideas in this book, you can expect to

- feel better about how you look, which in turn affects how good you feel about yourself and your life

- appreciate what is unique about you

- shake off gloomy thoughts about yourself

- care for yourself like someone you love

- be able to withstand criticism from others and negate harsh words that have hurt you in the past

- have altogether more confidence in yourself.

So, let's begin.

How To Use This Book

"You Are Beautiful! 53 Easy Ways To Love Your Imperfect Self" has 53 key confidence-boosting strategies. Please don't try to do them all at once. You'll get much further much faster by taking things a few steps at a time.

Start by reading through the whole book. It's designed to be practical and deliberately short so you can quickly get to the best way for you to move forward and take action.

Pick two or three strategies that resonate most with you and play with those ideas in your mind. Put them into practice, see them working and then pick one or two more. That way you will enjoy an almost instant boost to your confidence, and these early results will give you the motivation to continue.

You absolutely don't have to work through all of the strategies. If one or two don't appeal or don't apply to you, feel free to leave them and pick something else. Just be aware that it is sometimes the strategies that you are most resistant to, the ones you instantly dismiss, that you need the most. But you can always come back to them later and review how you feel about them.

By working through the book a few steps at a time in this way, you'll have a personal plan for feeling better about how you look in the shortest possible time. Don't get me wrong, it does take action on your part to implement the strategies that will make a difference to you, but the results are worth it. You will love feeling more confident about your image.

WAIT! A Gift For You!

Would you like more confidence in all parts of your life?

Do you want to feel better about yourself in every way?

"You Are Beautiful! 53 Easy Ways To Love Your Imperfect Self" focuses on feeling great about how you look and being one hundred percent comfortable with your self-image. But if you are generally low in self-esteem, your lack of confidence can affect every area of your life, including your career, your relationships and your happiness now and in the future.

As a thank you for taking a look at "You Are Beautiful! 53 Easy Ways To Love Your Imperfect Self", you can answer one quick survey question about confidence and get a FREE downloadable copy of my book "Rock-solid Confidence Step By Step: How To Be Confident And Happy With Yourself" (which is available in paperback priced at $9.99).

This book is a step-by-step guide to having more general confidence in your life, and if you couple that with the strategies in this book, your confidence really will sky-rocket in every way.

Visit the link below and take the one-question survey to get your FREE book!

http://lovefromana.com/moreconfidence

Now let's really get started.

FEEL MORE BEAUTIFUL

1

Go On A Media Diet

From a very young age, you have been force-fed hundreds of thousands of media images which show you the perfect woman with perfect legs, stomach, butt and breasts, not to mention the perfect face and hair - the kind of images that sell products, magazines and movies.

No doubt you have also seen endless articles about how to look good, that urge you to buy this diet, that dress or a whole bathroom cabinet full of beauty products so you can attain that perfect look for yourself.

They are all just selling you a pitch, their sneaky tactics have worked, and they have robbed you of your natural confidence in your own unique look.

If you can't get the thought of those perfect images out of your mind and how different they are from you, then the best thing to do is to stop feeding your brain with them.

Now before you panic about cutting yourself off from some of the activities you love, hold on a moment.

I know you might not want to give up your favorite shows, magazines and going to the movies, and yes, though that would undoubtedly help, it IS a bit harsh just so you can feel better about yourself. If you stopped all access to them, you'd probably feel like a dieter forbidden ever to touch chocolate or fries again. You would want to indulge in them more than ever. And in any case, it's almost impossible to cut yourself off completely. After all, there are billboards, newsstands and TV sets everywhere that will catch your eye.

So if you love these things, or you can't avoid them, there is an alternative.

What you can do is protect yourself against the THOUGHTS you have when you see them.

That's because it's not the images at fault. They don't do you any harm at all. It's the thoughts you have when you see them that create the damage.

You know the kind of thoughts I mean - the "She's so beautiful. I'll never look as good as her. No one will ever love me because I'm so ugly" kind.

The answer is to stop at the "She's so beautiful" thought, if you can't avoid seeing the pictures altogether.

Like A Painting Or Landscape

Look at the images as you might look at a beautiful painting or landscape. You enjoy these things for their own sake. You have to learn to do that with images of beautiful women too.

You need to be aware that these beautiful women with porcelain skin and perfect figures are just images. The women portrayed are generally attractive - I grant you that - but they are not perfect. They used to say that the camera never lies, but these days it does.

The photographer knows how to use lighting and lenses to make the subject look her best. Then, on top of that, the images are airbrushed and manipulated in an editing program like Photoshop to give the best possible picture of beauty that ever walked the earth.

It doesn't matter if the woman has a spotty chin or went on an all-night bender instead of getting her beauty sleep. The skin is made smoother and all kinds of wrinkles, blemishes and discoloration are removed. And then she is made thinner, her waist is made smaller and her breasts bigger or smaller or more pert depending on the perfect "look" the photographer is going for. Her cellulite, muffin top and bony areas are smoothed out. Everything can be "corrected" with image manipulation these days.

As for TV and movies, they use all sorts of makeup, lighting and camera tricks, not to mention body doubles, to make celebrities look good, so much so that movie stars need an army of hairdressers, makeup artists, personal trainers, and wardrobe experts to make sure they don't look a hundred times worse in real life.

So, if you compare yourself with the images of these women, you are comparing yourself with a fantasy, a woman who doesn't exist anywhere on the planet. You can't measure up. Of course you can't. Not even the woman in the movie or who has had her photograph taken measures up! So don't even try.

Now when you come across beautiful images, you can relax. Enjoy the celebrity gossip. Enjoy the (often weird) fashion choices on models. Enjoy the composition of the pictures brightening up the magazine. Enjoy the articles. Enjoy the movies. And don't let them worry you one little bit.

Soon you'll understand what is gorgeous about you.

2

Avoid Comparing Yourself

Perhaps you understand that the media show unrealistic images of perfect women. But you're still not satisfied with yourself. You say to yourself, "It's not just the magazines. The girls and women I see every day are all younger, thinner, and more beautiful than me. I can't even measure up in real life."

But that's just not true. You see women who are making the most of themselves – that's true – and there will always be someone who is younger, prettier and thinner than each of us, but that does not mean you are not beautiful in your own right.

And if you talked to those women, you would find out that every single one of them doubts her own attractiveness and feels she doesn't measure up in some way or another to the idea of perfection she holds in her mind.

Thoughts like that are pure poison to your peace of mind and your confidence. This kind of comparison makes you feel like you are in some kind of competition where there are winners and losers. And if you are not confident about your looks, then no doubt you feel like a loser most of the time, inadequate and anxious about your appearance. But there is no such competition in real life. Every woman is an island when it comes to looks.

Beauty is not a standard you have to attain. It's something you can embrace about yourself. There's not one perfect hair color or shape. Every woman has something unique and beautiful about her, even if there are features she doesn't like about herself. To boost your confidence, focus on you and your own special look and not on how that compares to other women.

3

Bring Out Your Uniqueness

If you have been used to comparing yourself with others, or with some ideal you had in your mind, and feeling that you fall short, it's worth spending some time thinking about yourself and what is special about you.

As teenagers, we want to be one of the pack and look just the same as everyone else so that we don't stand out at all. We do far too much comparing at that age. But as an adult, a beautiful woman in her own right and confident in her looks, it's better if you don't look like a clone. It doesn't mean that you have to dye your hair green or start wearing off-the-wall outfits (unless that is what you want), it just means emphasizing what is special about you.

If you can bring out your personality in how you look, you will feel really comfortable in your own skin and you'll have confidence in the image you're putting out there. That means thinking about the type of woman you are and matching that with the hair style, clothes and possibly makeup and jewelry you choose.

Women with style and confidence do this without thinking, but it doesn't have to come naturally to you. You can work on this over time and get the help of a personal stylist if you need to. (You can often book a session with a stylist for free in larger department stores.) You will have to do the thinking about what kind of woman you are though. No one can do that for you.

Consider the type of look that matches the real you. Perhaps you are romantic or fun-loving? A bit zany or conservative? Sporty or practical? You will have to adapt a little for different situations in your life and special occasions, but you can still show the "essential you" in your choices.

Most women have a whole closet full of clothes that have nothing to do with who they are. Many will be sale bargains and items plucked from the racks at the last minute in panic for a particular occasion, or things they just bought without thinking how much the item suited their personality.

You don't need a whole new wardrobe to feel confident. Just gradually replace the things that are not really you with things that bring out who you are. Experiment with makeup if you wear it and talk to your hair stylist next time you are due a haircut.

You will be amazed at how much confidence you get from feeling that the image you are putting out there is just right for you.

4

Find The Good

It's important to focus on your good points when you want to have confidence, but don't just focus on them, take delight in them. Yes, delight!

What do you appreciate and love about you? What are you most confident about? Make a list of those things. It's a great reminder for when you are feeling down about how you look.

What if you don't like anything about yourself? Maybe you don't think you have any good points. But I can tell you two good points right away.

The first is your eyes. Eyes are always beautiful, and they are also unique to you. They have color and character. They show your personality. They show what you find attractive, whether it is the man you love, a beautiful painting or a new dress. They show whether you are happy or sad.

The second thing about you that I know is beautiful is your genuine smile, the one that reaches your eyes. You see how important your eyes are! If your smile is genuine, your eyes twinkle and people warm to you when your smile is meant for them.

With no good points other than your eyes and your smile you can get through life with confidence because looking people in the eye and smiling mean they react positively to you. You have a kind of graceful charm that the woman looking at her feet and scowling does not. But everyone can smile and mean it. Practice having a few words and a genuine smile for everyone you come across. You will be amazed at what that does for your confidence.

Other great things about you

As well as your eyes and your smile, there will be many other attractive parts of you that you take for granted because you focus on what you dislike about your looks.

I don't know what you like about yourself or what you don't, but work on increasing the list of things you like. If you already started a list with your thoughts above, add to it. If you didn't, start one. Go into details when you write down your good points. And don't just read the list when you're feeling ugly. Read it often.

No point is too small for your list. Do a top-to-toe survey of yourself looking for things to admire. I guarantee that if you do, there will be quite a few things you do actually like about you.

For example, "I love the soft skin at the top of my thighs. I love the way tendrils of hair curl down my neck when I have my hair up. I love the rosy color of my lips. I love my ankles."

Whatever you have on your list, compliment yourself on it. Love yourself to bits.

5

Highlight It

Most women focus too much on the negative aspects of their appearance. They see only the flaws and take any beautiful features for granted. So once you decide on your good points (see Strategy 4), make the most of them so that they become the focal point of your look.

Don't hide your beauty away, display it. For instance, if you have nice hair, don't tuck it away in a ponytail or under a hat, make sure it's visible. If you have a great figure, you can't wander around in the nude, but you can display a little hint of cleavage and wear figure-skimming clothes that show off your shape.

Use clothes, accessories and makeup to draw attention to the best parts of you, and that way, few will notice the parts you're anxious to hide.

6

Enjoy Being You

If you've always hated how you look and wish you were someone else, perhaps your favorite celebrity, then it's time to stop those thoughts because you are missing out on a huge amount of fun and pleasure when you don't enjoy being you.

If you forget about how you look for a moment, and just think of all the things you love in the world – not just people, but also places, and possessions, things you love to do, movies, TV shows and people that make you laugh, skills you have that make you feel good, things that give you a boost – you'll realize the whole cornucopia of things that together make you unique and that you can be happy about.

Then think about all the unique character traits you have – the things that make your friends and family love you, the parts of you that get you through a bad day and still laugh at your guy's jokes, the daredevil you that makes you want to do your own thing and forget about what "they" expect of you - and you have a whole heap more to feel good about.

You are this wonderful unique person in character and personality, not just in looks. With all your eccentricities, all the things that make you YOU, how could you fail to love yourself? You are the sum total of all the things you like, all the funny thoughts in your head. You are a perfect you and would be a misfit in anyone else's life and body.

In fact, how you look is a unique amalgamation of your history. Firstly, you have genes from your family, and unless you don't know your birth parents, you probably recognize pieces of those you love in you – whether it's your mom's thick glossy hair or your dad's blue eyes. Secondly, it shows the unique life you have lived, whether that is stretch marks from a pregnancy, scars from when you fell out of a tree when you were ten, or a lifelong love of chocolate bars and ice cream.

Embrace everything that makes you the individual you are. Enjoy the wonderfulness of you. Remember your face and body are not separate parts of you to be hated and despised.

24

They are part of the whole wonderful package that is you, a part of the whole picture. You are not just a body and you never will be.

Practice acknowledging that you enjoy being you - because deep down you do! - and if you struggle with this, act as if you enjoy being you and before you know it, it will be true!

7

Be Your Own Best Friend

Once you have a list of all the great things about you and what is unique, I want you to start being a proper friend to yourself.

It's easy to slip into the habit of criticizing parts of you that you don't like over and over until you have a permanent dialog running in your head that gets you down and destroys your confidence.

It is unbelievable how much damage you can do to yourself with mean thoughts

- You're so fat.

- Look at that stomach – it's hideous.

- Why can't you be more like...,

- No one will ever look at you

- I expect he'll go off you soon, you're so ugly

Would you ever say those things to a friend you love? Would you even think them about a friend?

I don't think so. So why on earth would you do that to yourself? You should be the most important person in your world, the one you want to love and protect above all others. You should keep yourself feeling as safe and secure as you possibly can and want yourself to feel loved, happy and confident.

So what is the purpose of all the mean talk?

Sometimes it's just a bad habit you have acquired somewhere along the way. Often criticizing yourself is a form of self-protection. You criticize yourself first before anyone else can.

Or you don't want to be disappointed and so you give yourself reasons why you might not succeed and why things might not work out the way you hope. And lo and behold, they often don't work out. And that's not because you don't have the ability to succeed, but because you have the wrong mindset to take yourself anywhere that might be slightly out of your comfort zone.

To get on in the world, to make friends, to get the guy you want, you need to push yourself a bit, and you'll find it so much easier to do that pushing if you are not battering yourself into the ground with self-criticism.

So from now, on whenever you catch yourself being less than a friend to yourself, stop. Firmly resist indulging in any sort of pity party and make yourself admire something about yourself whenever the "critical you" shows her face.

Here are some simple rules to live by. Although they are simple to understand, you may find them hard to follow at first, but the more you catch yourself falling foul of them and stop yourself breaking them, the easier you'll find it to get out of the habit of being your own worst enemy.

- Never, ever, ever speak harshly to yourself.

- Forgive yourself if you get things wrong.

- Be gentle when you don't look your best.

- Accept yourself exactly as you are.

- Tell yourself often how good you look.

8

Change Your Labels

One of the things you can do to start being your own best friend is to change the labels that you use for yourself. You may be used to thinking of yourself as the shy one or the woman with no sense of style, the fat one among your friends or the one who never gets the guy. A label like this, used over and over again, undermines your confidence and self-esteem, and the more you think it, the more entrenched the whole idea becomes.

Choose some labels for yourself that are both true and uplifting. You're not the fat one, you're the one with great curves and beautiful red hair. You're not the one who lacks style, you're the woman with a flirty personality exploring her style options.

Use your positive personality traits and physical characteristics to build a positive word picture of yourself. And tell yourself often who you are. You don't need to be stuck with one description. Try one on for size and adapt it if it doesn't quite seem to fit and as you change.

This strategy goes well with being your own best friend and stopping the habit of criticizing yourself because it's sometimes easier to replace a bad habit than it is just to stop it. Good thoughts about yourself can be used to squeeze out the critical ones.

9

Challenge Your Ugly Thoughts

If you catch yourself being pessimistic and particularly down on yourself, listen to the statements you are using and deliberately challenge them. Ask the right questions to get the truth. For example, after a bad date with a guy who didn't seem very interested in taking things further, you might be saying to yourself something like this, "Nobody fancies me. I'm so fat, I'll never find anyone."

If someone else said that to you, you'd be shocked and annoyed, and you'd probably argue the point. But because you're saying it to yourself, you believe every word.

So pretend someone else said it (or give that critic a name like "your inner bitch") and challenge it. You are sure to find untruths, exaggerations and negative interpretations in there. Ask things like

- Is that really true?

- How do I know that for certain?

- Am I making too much of one incident?

- Am I making assumptions?

- Am I taking things personally when it may not be anything to do with me?

- What could be another explanation? And another?

- What would a good friend say to me about it?

Here's how you might refute that "Nobody fancies me…" statement.

- Perhaps you were not his type, but does one guy's view mean you're not right for any guys out there? Of course not!

- Has no one ever found you attractive? What about all the guys in the past? Even if you're not aware of any in particular, there are bound to be some!

- In any case, could you make yourself more attractive if you wanted to? Of course, you could.

- Could there have been other reasons why he wasn't interested? Perhaps he wasn't looking for the same things in a relationship as you? Maybe he was on the rebound and not really ready for dating?

- Why are you so sure you'll never find anyone? There are women of all shapes and sizes finding love every day.

Don't let an ugly statement go by unchallenged, and make sure you bring out the lack of truth in what you're saying to yourself. You won't notice every statement you make like that, especially if you are used to making them, but the more you spot and challenge them, the more confident you will feel over time.

10

Don't Join In

There's one thing worse than criticizing yourself in your head and that's when you say those things out loud and complain to others about your looks, pointing out what you see as your flaws.

It seems to be almost expected that when women get together, they moan about their hair or their skin or their bodies.

Don't join in the moan fest. Voicing your insecurities is not going to make you feel better about yourself at all. You're just reinforcing the idea that how you look is unacceptable and it eats away at your confidence.

Not only that, but other women feel that if you are critical of your own body, you must be critical of them too, particularly if, for example, your friend is larger than you and you are going on about your weight. Or you are saying that you feel like a lazy slob because you didn't go for a run today and she doesn't exercise. What must you think of her?

Not only do women get together and moan about their bodies all the time, making body hatred seem normal, even expected, they even log onto social media so they can publicly declare they feel fat or they pigged out. It seems totally self-obsessed to everyone else, not to mention boring.

Even if you're not the one that starts the body-bashing, don't join in with your own flaws just to be polite or show empathy. You are damaging yourself that way, and you're not helping your friend. Tell her how wrong she is and what's great about her. It's a much better way of making her feel better.

And if you're ever tempted to go on about your fat thighs or stomach (or whatever you're not happy with) to a guy, make yourself stop before you start. He hates it when you do that. If he agrees with you, you're devastated. If he reassures you, you don't believe him. He can't win. Also, if you keep going on about what's wrong with you, he might just start noticing what he hasn't noticed before, and you'll be less attractive in his eyes.

All that negative talk has to stop. It's unkind to you and everyone else listening. It's tedious. It's unnecessary. It gets you nowhere. Just don't do it.

11

Accept Compliments Graciously

When someone gives you a compliment, the only response you need is "thank you" and a smile. If you want to add anything you can say, "That's a really nice thing to say" or "I'm pleased you noticed" or "I just got it today" or whatever is appropriate. Whatever you do, don't try to deny that there's any truth in the compliment!

So many women start to explain why they are only as good as they are because of this or that or deny the whole idea that they could be worthy of praise.

It's really insulting the compliment-giver not to accept a compliment at face value. You're really saying he or she has poor taste if you start arguing against the compliment. If your friend raves about your new shoes you hunted high and low for, that's great news. If your guy loves your dress or your hair or your sexy body, be happy about it and smile!

12

Admire What You Can Do

We are living, breathing objects. We're not flat two-dimensional photographs to be gawked at, snapshots in time. When you think about all the things your body does for you, it is truly wonderful. The whole heart beating, breathing, digesting, moving, thinking, imagining, laughing, crying wonder of you is truly something magnificent and not to be taken lightly.

Appreciate the inner workings of your body as you go about your day. Your physical form allows you to move about so much, to enjoy so much, to get so much done, and it does exactly what it is supposed to do 24 hours a day, 365 days a year. Marvelous, isn't it?

Yet we take it all for granted and berate it for being ugly!

Madness!

If you're feeling less than confident about any part of you, praise and love it instead for what it can do. Your body allows you to experience the world with all your senses. The legs you hate get you from place to place. Those wobbly arms and soft stomach let you comfortably cuddle your kids or your guy. And your smile can light up a room, if you let it.

Your body is strong and functional in so many ways. Giving yourself credit for what you can do with your body can make you more confident about it and will encourage you to direct fewer hateful thoughts towards it. Even if your body is less than healthy and doesn't work as well as other bodies, it keeps you alive and lets you do whatever you CAN do. Love it to bits and you'll feel much better about yourself.

Your body is a blessing. See it that way.

13

See Exercise As A Gift

Never use exercise as a way to punish yourself. There's no need to run five miles because you ate a proper meal. If you exercise, do it not because it changes your shape but because you want to give yourself the gift of good health and feeling on top of the world.

If you choose an activity that you enjoy (think dancing or ice-skating or window-shopping if the gym is not for you), then you will benefit from the very first session. Your feeling of well-being will increase and stress levels will decrease. You'll have fun and you'll be showing yourself what your body is for, and that is moving not just admiring or berating!

Exercise is worth doing simply because of the way it increases your confidence in what you can do and lets you see your body in a more positive light. It may be a while since you experienced the sheer joy and satisfaction that comes from something like running in the fresh air, riding or swimming. But you don't have to even do that. If you can't face organizing anything more complicated, put on a pair of comfortable shoes and walk. Even 15 minutes a day will improve your mood and confidence in yourself.

14

Ignore The Scale

It's amazing how much power many of us give to a figure on the scale.

It has the ability to make us happy or give us a bad start to the day. It gives us permission to eat or tells us we should be starving ourselves. But it's only a number and has no real significance. It can't make you fat overnight. It can only make you feel fat overnight.

So why give it the power to make you feel bad about yourself?

If you are trying to get in shape, it will take you on a roller-coaster of emotion, yet your weight fluctuates for all kinds of reasons that are unrelated to fat loss such as

- the clothes you are wearing

- where on the floor you place the scale

- what kind of surface you place the scale on

- the time of day

- the time of the month

- how much salty food you consumed recently and therefore how much water you're retaining.

Instead of letting the scale have all the power, listen to your body.

Focus on being healthy and eating the kinds of food your body wants in quantities that leave you neither stuffed full nor starving. By treating your body with respect like that, you will probably be more successful at losing weight permanently than you have ever been from any starvation diet. And you'll certainly feel better and more confident without subjecting yourself to the tyranny of the scale.

15

Stop Judging

No woman is perfect. We all have our faults, and it can help to realize that fact when you are giving yourself a hard time.

You may compare yourself and see women who are younger and prettier than you, even though Strategy 2 talks about not doing so, but you may also be tempted to try and gain comfort from those who you think are less attractive than you.

Many women spend their time criticizing other women. They look at other women's bodies. They compare clothes and hair. They notice details, including faults.

While this helps redress the balance a bit and makes you feel that you and your looks are normal, it doesn't really help you in the long run. By getting into the habit of criticizing the women around you, your brain starts believing that others spend their time criticizing you. You think everyone's mind works like that. It doesn't!

Guys, for one, rarely notice the type of things that women do. They will notice great legs and totally miss that someone has frizzy hair in the rain. They are just not wired that way.

Confident women don't do this either. They don't need to point out the faults in others to make themselves feel better. Their feeling of confidence is based on their own unique look and not how they compare to others.

When you criticize other women, even in your head, all you're doing is making yourself feel insecure because you expect that everyone is noticing YOUR faults. And if you bitch with your girlfriends about other women, you're reinforcing the idea that people are noticing what is wrong with you and making your girlfriends insecure too. Don't do it.

Even criticizing the celebrities you admire so much when they're caught in the occasional ugly photo or outfit is a bad idea. It might make you feel superior momentarily, but it will have a dampening effect on your confidence over time. It just makes you feel that it's unacceptable to have cellulite or rolls of fat or a bad hair day and that when you do, you should hide away and not be out in public to suffer ridicule.

Try hard to fight the tendency to compare and criticize. Here's an easy way to get into a more positive groove:-

For every person you come across, on the bus, at work, in a bar or cafe or store, look for two positive things to THINK about their appearance. There's no need to say anything unless you want to spread your positive message with a sincere compliment now and again. But you'll be so busy looking for positive things, that you will forget to criticize. Not only will it make you feel better about your body, but it will also make you feel that both you and the world are nicer than they ever were before. Win-win all round!

If your friends tend to be super critical and that makes you feel insecure, steer the conversation elsewhere whenever they start. You can tell them you're reading this book about how to feel more positive about yourself, so you've decided to stop criticizing anyone else. They'll feel better for it too.

16

Realize How Little Others Notice

No matter how much you and your friends criticize other women, you can bet that you are criticizing yourself more than anyone else and noticing more flaws in your own appearance than you can find to talk about on anyone else.

It is just like when you lose a few pounds, your clothes feel better and you feel good, but everyone else is oblivious to any change in you. You have to lose a significant amount of weight before anyone notices. Ten pounds here or there is trivial and invisible to anyone else. They liked you before, they still like you now.

If you have created standards in your head of what is acceptable and what is not, trying to meet those standards and failing just gives you constant blows to your confidence.

Think about whether anyone would even notice if you achieved the goal you are working so hard on. Do you notice or care when friends lose ten pounds? If no one would even notice whether you achieved whatever it is you want to achieve with your appearance, don't stress about it. You can still have goals without beating yourself up about your progress in achieving something insignificant.

17

Make The Mirror Your Friend

Mirrors (and shop windows) seem to draw those of us with little confidence in our looks like moths to a flame. What do you do when you look in the mirror? Are you secretly checking yourself for faults, afraid of what you will see?

Many of us only notice our imperfections when we look in the mirror. We see the nose we don't like, not the friendly, smiling face that others see. We see the wobbly stomach or thighs, not the sexy, curvaceous lady that makes men want to get close.

It's time to change your relationship with your reflection.

Make the mirror your friend and never be frightened by it again.

How do you do that?

Let yourself look in the mirror with the eyes of someone who loves you – that's right – you! Don't judge or criticize. Just love yourself – all of you. We are so used to seeing imperfect fragments. You need to see yourself as a whole unique human being.

Gaze into your eyes and feel love and compassion for yourself. If you can do this for five minutes a day, it will have a remarkable effect on how you feel about yourself.

18

Quit Checking

Apart from the five minutes you spend with your mirror if you want to try Strategy 17, quit checking your appearance all the time.

Of course, you'll need a mirror to apply makeup, and a quick glance in a full-length mirror before you leave the house is a good idea to make sure your outfit looks good, but you don't need to keep checking your face and body all day long in every mirror and store window you see.

Constantly checking does not help your confidence, especially if you tend to focus on a part of you that you dislike. It just fuels your hatred. When you catch yourself doing it, stop, and deliberately switch your focus to something else unrelated to your appearance. For example, think about the day ahead, or someone you love, or your plans for an exciting future.

19

Pamper Yourself

Caring for your face and body with great treatments is one way of showing your subconscious how much you value yourself and your body. It will make you feel good and reduce stress. Some treatments will also make you look better.

But don't pamper yourself with the attitude of perfecting yourself so that you look great to others. Care for yourself because you know you are worth it. It doesn't matter if these things make you look any better as long as you feel pampered and loved. Try a mixture of treatments and include some that don't change how you look, but just how you feel about yourself. Some great treatments to try are

- Indian head massage

- full body massage

- flotation tank

- manicure

- pedicure

- daily skin care regimen

- yoga lesson

- deep cleansing facial

- long soak in a warm bath with a few drops of essential oil.

If you have a tiny budget, you can do many of these treatments yourself. And if you need products for your treatment, you can usually find something in your price range.

For example, you could buy yourself a bottle of beautifully perfumed body lotion or, if you can't afford that, the best lotion you can afford from your local drugstore. What matters is that you lovingly apply it.

See how loved and lovable you feel after you have had a good massage or other beauty treatment. Try to remember that feeling in your less confident moments. You are beautiful. You are worthy of care and good treatment.

20

Don't Ignore What You Don't Like

When it comes to pampering treatments, don't avoid the parts of yourself that you don't like. Give them special loving attention instead.

When you're looking in the mirror, gaze intently at that part of you with love and compassion, and decide what treat you could provide to make up for all the hatred you have sent its way. For example:

- If you dislike any part of your face, go for a professional facial and see each part treated lovingly, or try a home facial and care for your whole face yourself.

- If you hate any part of your body, a massage is a good idea. You can give yourself a massage with lotion, paying particular attention to the least favorite parts of your body, have a professional massage or ask someone who loves you to give you a soothing rub.

- If your feet or hands are the object of your loathing, try a professional manicure or pedicure.

- If it's your hair that causes you to freak out, a deep conditioning mask would be a great way to give your hair a treat.

Love your whole self, not just the parts of you that you consider acceptable to the world. The whole of you is acceptable. You are the only one who has an issue with any of you. No one else gives two hoots about your flaws!

21

Make Peace With The Lines On Your Face

Your face is like a map of your character and all your experiences. Don't get upset that you have a few wrinkles or lines. Cherish the fact that you have experienced life.

If you don't have a few crinkles at 30 and a few more each decade later, it looks as though you have had no life and have no personality. Imagine a seventy- or eighty-year-old woman with a completely smooth face. Is that attractive? No, it would look fake even if it could be achieved.

Of course, if lines upset you, you can have work done, but I'm advocating that you don't try to blot out the past or your age. Own it and feel good about yourself for having enjoyed life this far.

You're not a movie or TV star worried about being passed over because the powers that be favor younger women. That is another one of those media games that we shouldn't buy into. It's sad to see celebrities who feel they have to get rid of every line. Often you see their faces stretched over their bones so much by cosmetic surgery that their features are distorted.

I'm not saying that you shouldn't care for your skin. Look after it by moisturizing and protecting it from the sun. Just don't berate it for showing the results of years of joy and laughter or even concern. Those lines show your humanity and your willingness to participate in life to the full so celebrate that.

22

Feel Connected

Being mindful about what you and your body need is another way of caring for yourself and showing your subconscious you are worth it. Children instinctively know what they need. If they are hungry, they soon let you know. If they are tired, they lie down and fall asleep anywhere. As adults, we lose much of that, often eating based on scheduled mealtimes or greed and resting only once there's nothing on TV we want to see and we're finished surfing the net. Even when we are ill, we often force ourselves to keep going. It's as if our body is an inconvenience getting in the way of our life.

But when you start being mindful of your body, what it needs and what it likes, and you start paying it the respect it deserves as a finely tuned mechanism, you are showing yourself that you are worth caring for and loving.

Some ways to be more connected with what you need are

- eating when you are hungry and stopping when you are satisfied (rather than uncomfortably full)

- enjoying your food and savoring every mouthful so that you don't mindlessly eat too much

- drinking when you are thirsty

- stretching or moving when your muscles are feeling tight

- going to bed or taking a nap when you are tired

- having at least one day a week when you allow yourself to wake up without an alarm clock

- taking a bathroom break when you need to. (Don't put it off and be uncomfortable just because you are busy)

- wearing clothes that fit and are comfortable

- choosing shoes that you can easily walk (even run!) in, unless you're just hopping in and out of a taxi or on a special night out

- taking it easy and looking after yourself when you are ill

- relaxing when you are stressed

- singing when you feel like singing and dancing when you feel like dancing.

If you listen to your body and follow what it is asking for, you'll look better and you'll feel better. You will also be truly treating yourself as the precious person you are, and that will help your confidence and feeling of self-worth day in and day out.

23

Dress Well

Are you dressing as someone who doesn't think much of herself? Whether you are at home or out and about, always wear clothing that makes you feel good about yourself.

Why bother to dress well at home? You might think it doesn't matter and you might damage your good clothes, but it's a question of respecting yourself and how you look. You don't have to dress expensively to do jobs around the house, but there's no reason to look a mess and wear dirty, stained clothing either. You are worth nice clothes. Show yourself you're worth it. Never wear anything you hope no one will see you in or clothes that make you feel self-conscious and you'll never feel humiliated or lack confidence because of what you're wearing.

Clothes can reveal a weak body image or they can be used to enforce a good one. If you have a healthy body image, you will naturally choose comfortable, well-fitting clothes that suit you and your individual style. The right clothes don't overwhelm you. People notice how attractive you are, not just what you're wearing.

Looking good in your clothes will give you so much more confidence than wearing baggy sweats, worn, stained clothing or items which don't suit or even fit you anymore. It's worth putting some thought into your wardrobe.

Choose Clothing That Fits

If you choose clothing that fits and is comfortable, it will help you feel a healthy connection with your body (see Strategy 22). You'd think that no one with any sense would torture themselves with clothes that dug into them all day, right? But that's what many of us do when we squeeze into the wrong size clothing, afraid to acknowledge that we no longer fit into the size we used to.

It's much better to dress the body you have (and look good) than the one you wish you had (and have lumps and bulges all over). Choose figure-friendly, body-skimming clothes and you will feel much more confident. The size on the label does not matter - no one can see it.

Figure-friendly does not mean covering everything up. Don't choose loose, baggy clothing in the hope of disguising your shape. It doesn't fool anyone, and it won't make you look or feel confident if you are going about wearing a tent.

Be Yourself

Trying to hide your body is not the only way that you may show a lack of confidence when you dress. Perhaps you use another form of disguise that limits you, such as covering yourself top to toe in designer labels or wearing some kind of cult clothing where everyone looks the same (just think back to the punk era). But you are not a stereotype, so don't become one.

The clothes you choose are important in bringing out your uniqueness (see Strategy 3) so be mindful of that when choosing your confident look.

Your Shopping Strategy

Every time you buy something from now on make sure

- it is comfortable - so that you are not endlessly fidgeting with the neckline or the hemline

- it suits your personality and body shape

- it makes you feel attractive rather than dowdy or slutty

- it lifts the color of your face rather than makes you look like you need a good sleep

- you have the right things to go with it or are going to get them soon

- you would be happy to wear it bumping into your ex or arch rival.

It doesn't need to cost a fortune to look good. You can look a million dollars if you wear the right clothes, but you need to invest a bit of time working out what suits you. You can employ a personal shopper or simply spend ages trying on everything you like until you find clothes that are perfect for you. If you have a few outfits in your closet that you know you can call on to make you feel good when you need a boost, it can do wonders for your confidence.

24

Don't Forget What You Can't See

While you're considering your clothes, don't forget what you wear underneath your outfit. Although your undies are not usually visible to the world, you know you are wearing them. You shouldn't just care about having clean underwear for the unlikely event that you have an accident and end up in hospital like your mother taught you.

If you go about in panties that have lost their elastic and a badly fitting bra, you are showing yourself that you are not worth better. Treat yourself to lingerie you love and that suits your style, and you'll feel great even if you are the only one who knows about it.

The right underwear has the added bonus of making your clothes look better too. If you're wearing the wrong bra size or style of panties, they can create extra lines, lumps and bumps that you don't need. And a well-fitting bra can lift your whole figure (literally), so don't neglect this aspect of your appearance if you want to feel confident in your look.

25

Declutter It

One of the best ways to start feeling better about how you look is to get rid of any item of clothing that makes you feel ugly. It's surprising how many of these things we have hanging in our closets.

This includes

- items of clothing that look worn out even if they were once good

- things that no longer fit. If you really think you will slim into them, pack them away out of sight in the garage or attic. They are not something you want to have to look at every day.

- clothes you bought that never really suited you for one reason or another. Get those bad purchases out of your closet (sell them or donate them)

- things you never wear for any reason

- stained clothing.

Once you are rid of these things, you can organize what is left and see where there are gaps in your wardrobe and therefore items you need to buy once your budget allows.

And don't stop once you have decluttered your clothes. Also get rid of all those beauty products and gadgets you bought that were not quite right for you. If you don't use them, it's much better to get them out of your life so you can streamline your beauty routine and save time. Declutter your makeup bag too.

You may not think any of this will have much effect on your confidence, but we are all short of time. If you can grab an outfit that you know looks good in a couple of seconds and can do your hair and makeup in record time because you don't have to sort through a lot of things you don't need, it will save you running out of the house looking frightful when you are running behind, something that can affect your confidence all day. Once I went out wearing one navy shoe and one black shoe because I got ready in a rush and in the dark!

26

Understand
The Beauty Industry

While you're decluttering your beauty products, take a moment to reflect on why you have so many. Chances are you bought all those things you don't use because you believed an ad you saw somewhere that convinced you there was something slightly wrong with you. You suddenly saw a need for shinier hair, smoother skin, longer lashes, and just the right color of nail polish.

The beauty industry is selling a dream so that we buy their stuff. They care about profits, not about making you feel good about yourself. In fact, it is in their interests to make you feel insecure and in need of enhancement. You can feel perfectly fine before you see their ads and then "Whoosh!" a girl with amazing skin, body, hair or nails creates envy making you want to buy the product.

Start to recognize the marketing ploys and tricks of the manufacturers and don't believe everything you watch or read.

Create a simple beauty routine that works for you using the products that you need. Buy more when the product runs out. If you find a product that you think looks like it works better than the one you have, wait until the one you have is finished and then evaluate the new product. It's unlikely to make a discernible difference, but there's no harm in trying new things if you can afford them. Just don't expect miracles.

You don't need shelves full of products of every conceivable kind to be acceptable. You are fine right now. Remember this thought when you reach for your wallet. There is some conning going on, and your confidence will suffer if you believe the spiel. If you're tempted, ask yourself questions like

- Will a minuscule addition to the length of my lashes really make me more attractive?

- Will that moisturizer really make my skin so much smoother than it is now that everyone will notice?

- Will using that sea-green nail polish make anyone love me more?

I think you'll find the answer is "No" every time. Feel confident about your looks despite the beauty industry, not because if it. Remember they are dependent on you. You are not dependent on them.

27

Change If You Want To

Don't feel you NEED to change anything to feel good about yourself. In any case, there will be a lot of things about you that you can't change (or are unwilling to change). You are you, beautiful you, wonderfully human, scars, excess pounds and all.

But if it makes you feel better and more confident, there's no harm in changing those things that you can change, if changing doesn't affect your health and well-being (except for the better).

Here are some things you can do to feel better about yourself:

- Get a new haircut.

- Get your hair colored by an expert.

- Try an ultra-deep conditioning treatment.

- Begin an exercise or diet program.

- Smooth your skin with lotion.

- Look after your hands and feet.

- Get rid of unwanted hair on your face or body.

- Have a tooth-whitening treatment.

- Save up for invisible braces on your teeth.

- Buy some new pretty undies that fit perfectly.

Notice how there is overlap here with the strategy about taking care of yourself (Strategy 19). There's nothing wrong with making the most of what nature gave you. It's when you berate yourself for what nature gave you or for not doing as much as you possibly can to make the most of yourself that problems occur.

Remember, no one has endless time or money to keep up a 24-hour beauty routine. Very few of us have the willpower to keep our bodies in prime condition. Sometimes that's what we expect of ourselves and then give ourselves a hard time for not achieving the impossible. You'll never achieve perfection and you should never try.

But we can do those things that we have time for, the things that not only make us look good but also make us feel good. That's healthy! Feeling ugly because you have an extra layer of fat on your tummy is not.

One word of caution: don't do ANY of these things with the attitude of punishing yourself: "I'm a pig for eating that cupcake, I'd better go and spend an hour killing myself on the treadmill." Make the effort because you want to look after yourself, live to be 105 and enjoy the experience of making the best of yourself, as well as the results. Remember, exercise does not have to be punishing - it can be salsa dancing, surfing or ice-skating – and yes, even sex. Dieting does not have to be boring – it can be treating yourself to the very best foods – smoked chicken, lobster or exotic fruit.

Your body deserves the best you can give it, but there's no need to be so enthusiastic about being the best you can be that you hate the whole process.

Give yourself a break. Just don't let yourself go completely if you want to feel confident and good about yourself. There has to be a balance.

28

Get Expert Help

An expert can be invaluable when you want to make changes. Sometimes they are absolutely essential to the process, but they can also help when you're not quite sure what to do.

Have A Makeup Lesson

You don't have to wear makeup to feel confident about how you look, but most women like to wear a little, and it can definitely help emphasize your good points, so why not?

If you do want to wear makeup but you lack the skill to apply it well, book yourself in for a lesson with a professional makeup artist. Find out how to give yourself different looks that work for your lifestyle, such as a natural look for the daytime and weekends, a professional look for the office and a more glamorous look for evening.

Make The Most Of Your Hair

Don't underestimate the power of a good haircut (and perhaps color) in making you feel confident about how you look. Studies have shown that most women feel a "bad hair day" affects their confidence.

Choose your stylist with care – from personal recommendation if you can. And don't be afraid to ask for a consultation before taking the plunge with a new look. Take pictures of the kind of looks you like, and ask advice about whether they will suit your face shape and type of hair. Remember to take into account how much time you have for styling your hair each day (and how much skill).

When it comes to hair, as in many things, it seems that the grass is always greener on the other side of the fence. Curly-haired girls often want straight, sleek hair, whereas girls with straight hair would like to try bouncy curls at some time in their life. But resist the urge to move away from your natural hair type unless you're dead set on it. It will be much more difficult to manage if you go against the grain, and, in any case your natural hair type probably suits your face and personality.

What about color? Should you color your hair?

My take on this is that if you feel prettier and more confident with colored hair, then go for it. I have colored mine for years and feel better for it. It's a bit like makeup. There's no reason not to do it if it makes you feel better. Color can lift your complexion, catch the light and give your whole look a boost. Just make sure you can afford the cost and time you will need for keeping the color looking good. It's not going to help your confidence if your roots are always showing. Again, if you don't stray too far from your natural color, you will make things easier for yourself as far as maintenance is concerned. Roots will be less obvious close to your natural color than if you go dark to blond or vice versa.

Consult A Dermatologist

If you have a skin condition which affects your confidence, get the best professional help you can afford. I suffered severe acne as a teenager so I know how this can affect how good you feel about how you look. I grew out of it eventually, but meanwhile medication kept things in check and helped me feel better about myself. If budget is an issue, there are many drugstore products which will help with skin complaints, but be gentle on yourself and don't go treating your skin like it was the enemy. It needs love and care, not harsh treatment.

Other Professionals

There are so many types of professional help that it is a gargantuan task to create a list of every possibility, but if you know something is affecting your confidence and you believe an expert could help, seek one out. The kinds of experts you might think about consulting are

- dentists

- orthodontists

- personal stylists

- beauty therapists

- laser hair removal technicians

- alternative health practitioners

- nutritionists

- personal trainers.

If you have limited time and budget, you have to be selective, so think carefully about what will really help. Make sure you are not back in the mindset of aiming for impossible perfection. If something will make a big difference to how you look with no risk to your health and well-being, then investigate it, but never feel that it is something you have to do to be acceptable to others, or engage a professional in the spirit of hating yourself.

Be especially careful if you decide to put a cosmetic surgeon on your list of experts. Surgery is never without risk or pain. Many who have undergone procedures feel (and more often than you might expect actually look) worse than before their operation.

Before you decide, thoroughly investigate the benefits, risks, and side effects for the type of surgery you are looking at. Never see it as an easy option. Remember that you are not perfect before the surgery, and that you also won't be perfect after it. It may very well make more sense to work on your confidence than to go through the expense and pain of surgery.

84

29

Fix Confidence-Depleting Habits

Anything that affects your well-being and health, or your perception of yourself as a confident person in control of her life and habits, is well worth fixing. Some people manage to seem confident to others, but they are hiding a lot of issues and never feel good about themselves. But feeling confident is more important than looking confident. If you can break bad habits that affect your looks and how you feel about them (and sometimes your life), then you'll feel so much better about yourself.

Confidence-depleting habits are issues where professional help may speed up the process, and seeking help could be essential in cases where you are truly addicted.

What type of habits deplete your confidence?

Drinking To Excess

While a drink or two might make you feel temporarily more confident, relying on a crutch like that all the time is not the way to feel good about yourself long term. If you start needing to drink a lot to get through a night out, or you sometimes drink so much that you are out of control, it's time to think about cutting back your intake. Drunks are not attractive (except to predatory men), so do yourself a favor and put a lid on overdoing it. Your confidence can do without bloodshot eyes and alcohol on your breath the morning after the night before.

Starving/Binging

Addiction to food is pretty common and the trouble with food is that you can't stay away from it entirely. You have to eat!

Don't give yourself a hard time about being a few pounds overweight or eating too much now and again. But if you have an unhealthy relationship with food and you are in a cycle of hating your body so much that you are doing things like

- starving yourself

- eating huge amounts of food in one go so that you end up feeling ill

- making yourself throw up what you just ate

it's time to get some professional help to overcome your food issues. It's pretty much impossible to feel confident about your looks if you are going through this kind of thing. And it's difficult to break the pattern by yourself. Get help!

Smoking

You know the score. Smoking damages your health and your looks over time. Plus the smell of nicotine on your clothes and breath is off-putting, particularly to those who don't smoke. It's not easy giving up once you start smoking regularly, but if you do, it will give such a boost to your confidence and health that it will be worth the effort.

Recreational Drugs

The highs you get from a true feeling of confidence in yourself are much more valuable than any drug-induced euphoria that is swiftly followed by feeling awful. If you're taking any kind of drugs to get an artificial high, there's only one thing to do and that is to stop. Get help if you can't stop on your own.

Sleeping Around

You won't find any lectures here about how many guys you sleep with. That's a personal choice and nobody's business but yours. But if you are looking to get your feelings of self-worth and attractiveness from the number of guys you seduce, and it's not making you feel good, then it's time to take stock and think whether your behavior is working for you.

Feelings of confidence and self-worth need to come from inside your own head and not from what others think of you. Feeling beautiful just because a lot of guys want to sleep with you is not a sound basis for self-confidence.

30

Sit, Stand And Move Well

It's amazing how good posture can take years off your age and pounds off your weight. Walk, stand and sit up tall with your shoulders back and relaxed and you'll look and feel so much more confident than if you slouch. If you don't do this, remember that even if you are wearing an outfit that is stylish and perfect for you, poor posture will cancel out all the good effects.

Confident body language helps create a feeling of confidence in your mind. If your shoulders are sagging and your eyes are focused on the floor, you are going to look and feel down in the mouth. If you cross your arms and avoid looking anyone in the eye, you will look and feel defensive. But looking the world in the eye and maintaining a relaxed confident posture says to the world and your mind that you are happy to be wherever you are and can handle whatever is happening.

When your body language is confident and open, people react well to you and treat you better, and this in turn makes you feel better and have more confidence. Do everything you can to create that vicious (or in this case virtuous) circle.

All it takes is practice and noticing when your posture is poor so that you remember to correct it. If you catch yourself slouching, straighten your back hold your head up and move your shoulders back and down to open up your chest. Don't force the position. You should still feel relaxed. You're not a soldier on parade, just a woman holding herself well. If you catch yourself looking at the floor and avoiding eye contact, look up and smile. If you feel yourself getting defensive, uncross your arms and take the scowl off your face. When you start noticing poor posture, you may be dismayed at how much you have to correct yourself, but over time it will become a habit to sit, stand and move well.

31

Practice

It always helps you to be confident and self-assured if you know what you are doing. You feel more in control of any situation. This doesn't just apply to doing your job or managing your life, it can also make a difference to how confident you feel in your appearance.

If you want to feel confident in how you look, practice will help. In Strategy 30, we looked at how you sit, stand and walk, and your body posture. Practicing those things until they are second nature will help you enormously.

If you want to feel confident about your hair, practice various hair styles and see how they behave out in the real world where your hair may have to cope with rain, snow, humidity or heat. Practice with makeup until you have several "looks" that suit you and that work for the office, a party, a hot summer day etc. If you're not sure how to wear various accessories such as hats, jewelry and scarves, have fun experimenting in your bedroom at home before you go out.

Learn To Walk Again

This is totally optional, but one thing that can improve your confidence in how you look on a big night out is learning to walk in heels.

If you'd like to wear them, and love what they do for your legs, the secret is to practice. You can definitely get used to them and learn to walk elegantly in a pair of heels. Here are some tips:

- You need shoes that fit correctly and stay on your feet as you'll never learn to walk properly if they keep slipping off.

- Start with wedges or platforms and lower heels (two to three inches) until you get used to them, and then progress to stilettos and higher heels if you want to.

- Don't wear high heels every day. Give your feet a break and vary the heights of your shoes.

- Wear your heels at home until you feel confident enough to walk elegantly in them without falling over.

- Take smaller steps than you normally would.

- Practice on different surfaces (carpet, smooth flooring, sidewalk etc) and avoid getting your heels stuck in any crack, grid or grate. (This is not good for your confidence!)

Persevere and you'll soon get the hang of it. Walk tall and feel good in your heels!

32

Get In The Picture

Take a trip down memory lane and find pictures of yourself where you are happy and smiling and that give a good sense of who you are. Make an album with them. When you're feeling down, look through the pictures to see yourself looking but also feeling great.

If you have photographs that make you happy where you are doing something physical, be sure to include them to remind yourself of what your body is for. These could be photographs of you riding a horse, painting a picture, splashing in the waves or cuddling a child, for example. It doesn't really matter what you choose for your picture album as long as the images bring a smile to your face.

If you don't like having your picture taken because of how you look in them, remember typical photos taken by friends and family with no photography experience are not going to do you justice. Get a professional picture taken by a photographer who specializes in relaxed portrait photography.

You could even try a makeover package to get an idea of the looks that are possible for you. Studios specializing in makeovers usually offer makeup and hair styling (and sometimes clothing) to make sure you look great in your pictures. There is also quite a trend for sexy boudoir shots featuring soft lighting and lingerie.

If you're used to getting pictures you hate, you'll be surprised at the beauty the photographer brings out in you. It won't be fake like the pictures in magazines. The photographs will be flattering and show off your very essence, providing a great confidence boost by showing you how good you can look.

33

Be Your Own Trend

The idea of what makes a beautiful woman has changed over the centuries, and these days it changes from fashion season to fashion season, with different colors of hair, makeup or styles of eyebrow being the most sought after.

At the moment, slim is beautiful. Centuries ago it was better to have a bit more flesh on your bones. And current fashion always seems to favor youth over age, though these days movie stars who age gracefully get better press than those who fight against the signs of advancing years and have obvious surgery.

Accept that society has these views of beauty. You can't do much about that. But you don't have to adhere to these trends. They don't matter. You just have to like yourself and adopt your own style.

If you look at most women out and about, they don't conform to any sort of fashionable stereotype, but they can still look attractive in their own way if they look after themselves and dress well for their personality and body type.

Do the same and you will feel great about yourself, whatever the fashion and beauty magazines say about the latest trends. Be your own trend!

34

Accept Yourself

You don't have to be accepted by everyone to like yourself and feel confident in your looks. You will never please all of the people all of the time no matter what you do. So don't worry about what anyone else thinks. You are the one whose opinion counts. Make the most of yourself. Be who you want to be, present yourself as best you can and let everyone else worry about their own opinions.

People will judge you on how you look. You can't really get away from that. But don't let that get you down. Everyone has their prejudices, but they belong to the person who owns them and not to you.

For example, one individual will look at a person in glasses carrying a load of books and think, "Probably a geeky student with her head immersed in study." Another will think, "I bet she's interesting. I would love to have a conversation with her." One person will look at someone who is overweight and think she is probably friendly and cheerful with a relaxed attitude, and another will assume that she's out of control with food or lazy. And the skinny don't escape prejudice either. They may be thought of as anxious, even anorexic and highly strung, or lithe and athletic.

You can't do anything about other people and their perceptions until they get to know you and find out who you are. You know the kind of person you are inside and that is what counts the most. Accept yourself for who you really are. You are not your body and the impression it makes. You are one complex human individual and wonderful in yourself. Your body is just a receptacle that allows you to live in the world and do whatever you need to do. Love it for that.

35

Recognize The Real Source Of Dissatisfaction

If you are dissatisfied with your body so much that it is affecting your life, then look for the source behind your body hatred because it is unusual for happy and contented people to feel that way about themselves.

You may believe that you can't be happy because of your body and how you look, and you may even single out particular parts of you or aspects of your appearance to explain why you feel that way.

But if you could change that characteristic overnight, you'd feel momentarily happier, but it would not change a thing about how you feel long term. You would probably find something else about your appearance to focus on and be unhappy about.

So if you find yourself truly hating how you look, probe deeper. What is the real source of the discontent in your life? Work on that and when that improves so much that you are happier, you will feel much more confident about your image.

36

Set The Right Goals

After years of wanting to lose weight, dieters who actually achieve their goal rarely feel as good as they expect. Of course there's an achievement to celebrate. They like what the change does to their body. But it doesn't solve all their problems. They are still the same person. They still have insecurities. There are still parts of them that they haven't come to terms with and that they can't change. And a great life doesn't suddenly kick in with a weight loss of fifty pounds.

Researchers have found that achieving goals that give you a sense of accomplishment in your career, that enhance your health and relationships or that lead to personal growth give you much more satisfaction and happiness and more positive feelings about yourself than goals that only aim to change your image or are concerned with material gain. And confidence in yourself as a whole helps improve how you feel about your looks anyway, so it's all good.

If you are inclined to make "looking better" the focus of your life, realize that you will make very little impact by how you look and so much more with what you do. In the end, it is what you achieve during your life and not how you look that will bring you happiness.

There's no need to throw the baby out with the bathwater though. Why not have both goals - those which improve your image and those which improve your life? And if you can, tweak your image goals so that they focus on improving your health and well-being, your participation in life rather than just being all about how you look. For example, you could focus on your health rather than going on a punishing starvation diet when it comes to losing weight, and give all the clothes that don't suit you to charity rather than just "improving your wardrobe."

37

Leave No Gap

All around the world, there are women who are so busy or so preoccupied with other cares that they don't have the time to worry about how they look.

They are striving to do great things or just to feed their families. Whatever they are doing, they don't care that their neighbor has bigger breasts or a more pert bottom. They are not out buying products that will make no discernible difference to how they look. They are not pouring over the latest celebrity magazines or wondering whether blue or green is in this season. It just doesn't cross their mind.

I'm not saying you should give up on finding out about the latest in fashion and beauty trends if you find it interesting and fun. What I AM saying though is it should just be fun. Don't let it take over your life and make you obsessed with your own looks.

In some ways, it is almost a luxury to feel self-conscious about yourself. If there's no gap in your life, if you are busy accomplishing things, you leave no room for thoughts about your perceived flaws to creep in.

If you have enough time on your hands to spend thinking about yourself, you could easily change to become one of those women who is achieving great things or even just someone who keeps busy and has an active life.

If you find yourself obsessing over how you look, put it to one side and get busy!

38

Don't Wait

Focusing only on your image goals means you may be putting off living your life.

Don't do that!

You should always be aiming to live your life as you want to live it in the moment. Don't wait until you reach some goal with your appearance for your life to begin. The typical form this takes with women is needing to drop twenty or fifty pounds before getting on with something that will make a significant difference to their lives. For instance, they may put off going to college, applying for a promotion or dating because they don't think they are acceptable as they are.

The sad thing is that the more you live your life, the better you'll feel and the less fixated you'll be on the comfort that food brings.

This form of waiting can also take the form of denying yourself pleasure. ("I can't go on vacation until I look fantastic on the beach.")

Everything you do should be about what you want now, not what you'll only allow yourself to experience once you look a certain way. However you look, I guarantee it is perfect for living your life. Women everywhere, each with their own unique look, all shapes and sizes, are living great lives and enjoying every moment. Why wait for yours to start?

Imagine if you knew that nothing would ever change with your appearance, you were going to stay exactly the same as you are now, what would you still want to make sure you did with your life? How would you want to spend your time? Start doing that now. Your looks are not getting in your way. You are getting in your way. Living your life to the full will put a spring in your step and a sparkle in your eyes and you will be much more attractive and feel better about yourself than if you just wait for your life to start.

39

Be Aware Of What You Pay Most Attention To

Your thoughts naturally follow whatever you spend your time on and what you pay the most attention to. If you can't find it in yourself to love those parts of you that you don't like (Strategy 20), you'll need to try something else.

If you spend all your time trying to get rid of a few rolls of fat or frizzy hair or acne, or gazing at them in the mirror worrying that you'll never be attractive while they are present, then you will feel that they are the most significant part of you, completely missing all your good points and character traits.

Do what you can to fix those things if they bother you and are fixable, but don't make a big fuss about it. Simple routines you do consistently that become habits you don't have to think about are often the answer anyway to beauty problems that are fixable. If you can't find a simple solution, seek the help of a professional, or change your focus away from those problems and onto the things you like about you.

Too much time spent thinking about your perceived flaws means you can't help but feel that you are not good enough. To have confidence, focus on the great things about you. Take pride in them and feel good.

Work on changing your normal pattern of thinking so that whenever you start to dwell on something negative about yourself, you immediately switch to thinking about yourself in a positive way. See your face and body as a source of satisfaction, not something to complain about. If you do that consistently, it will become a habit that makes you feel good about yourself.

40

Forget The Past

People don't always keep their prejudices and nasty opinions to themselves. We have all had people say hateful things about us at some point in the past. But whatever someone has said about you, there's no need to keep it with you forever.

Being criticized about how you look is more common at school where kids can be cruel (although thoughtless adults often make devastating remarks too when we are growing up). If you are sensitive, you may keep going over those insults in your head and end up taking them to heart, reducing your confidence in how you look for a lifetime.

Think about the negative messages you are still carrying around in your head and where they came from. Why did those people behave so badly by criticizing you in that way? What was missing in their life? What were they trying to achieve by making you feel bad? Critical people generally lack confidence in themselves and find an outlet for their dissatisfaction by finding fault with others. They are not worth listening to once, never mind beating yourself up over again and again with their negative comments.

If the insults focused on something you can't do anything about, or you can't easily do something about, just shrug them off and get on with your life. If people feel the need to put you down, remember their criticism says more about their thoughtlessness, insecurity and bitchiness than it does about you. The best revenge is not letting it bother you. Replace their message with what you wish they had said, then focus on loving yourself using all the strategies in this book, not going over old ground again and again.

If something said way back in your past bothers you AND you can do something about it, still think twice before you change anything. What they criticize may be the very thing that makes you unique and stand out from the crowd. An example of this would be if you have red hair and freckles. Kids can tease mercilessly about something like that, so you might dye your hair and wear thick makeup, but this would actually reduce your beauty. The essence of you is in your beautiful red hair and freckles. Play them up, don't change them.

Write down any criticisms that still hurt you to this day. Get them all down on a sheet of paper and then symbolically burn that sheet (just don't burn your fingers or set fire to anything else in the process or you won't feel better!). Criticism only harms you if you let it get to you. Are you really going to let those bullies and thoughtless people from years ago get you down? I hope not.

Forget the past. It can only harm you if you let it.

41

Deal Decisively With Criticism And Teasing

If you are still subject to criticism and teasing as an adult (or misguided comments from friends and family), then you need a way to handle these things as soon as they happen to avoid continual blows to your confidence. You need a way to shut up the critics.

There's no need to think of any kind of argument to refute a rude and hurtful comment. You probably won't be able to think up a clever retort on the spot. But you can make the perpetrator realize that you are less than impressed by their remarks.

Raise your eyebrows and say something like, "How kind. Thanks for sharing your opinion." and walk off, or change the subject if you can't get away. They will be left speechless, knowing they are in the wrong. They will feel embarrassed for having made the comment, they may even apologize and will be less likely to repeat their behavior.

Remember these types of remarks are more likely to come your way from those who lack confidence themselves. It makes them feel better to criticize you. For a moment, it lets them feel superior. Don't let them get to you. Always have the attitude, "I don't need you to like how I look. I like myself." If they continue to bully you, then get them out of your life if you can. You are better off without them.

How you then react to the comments is up to you. Just like remarks you have been holding onto from your past (Strategy 40), you can take them on board and let them affect you (not recommended!), you can use them as motivation to change how you look (if that's what you want to do anyway) or you can forget them entirely and shore up your confidence in other ways.

Don't ever let people who are not even mature and evolved enough to keep their vicious thoughts to themselves affect you negatively. Your own good opinion of you counts for so much more than theirs.

42

Don't Give Single Opinions Too Much Power

Sometimes we give undue weight to criticism from one person. If someone criticizes something about you, it is the opinion of only one person. It's not a rejection by the whole world. We are too prone to accept the criticism of one spiteful person as the absolute truth while ignoring compliments from a whole group of people. Don't let yourself brood on what a vicious remark means and let it get you down. It just means that one person is a bitch!

If the opinion comes from someone you care about, criticism hurts more than ever. After all, you care about that person's good opinion.

The question is, in what spirit were the remarks made?

If they were meant to wound you, then it's time to reconsider your relationship and to cool things off. Confidence means loving yourself and not putting up with ill intent from those you care about. However, it may have been a clumsy attempt at teasing, to let you know that you are loved "warts and all." Let the person know that you are hurt and ask him or her to stop making remarks like that.

And don't put up with it if the criticism doesn't stop. It's up to you to set boundaries and make it clear what they are. Verbal bullying in relationships is just as undermining of your confidence and happiness as physical abuse.

43

Don't Take It Personally

It's one thing when you receive direct criticism about how you look, and we have looked at how you can deal with that, but so many of us react to any kind of sideways look or someone being short with us as implied criticism too.

It's rarely anything to do with you at all.

There are always multiple reasons why someone may react the way they do. Let's say you chat to a guy while waiting for drinks at the bar but he doesn't continue the conversation. Does it mean you're as attractive as a slug and no one will ever want to date you?

No! It's likely that he is already involved with someone, getting over a breakup, not interested in girls, or too shy to talk to you. Even if you are not his type, it doesn't mean that someone else won't find you hot.

Never assume the worst when you don't get the reaction you want in any given situation. Chances are it's not personal.

44

Learn From The Past

Although you should not dwell on negative remarks people made in the past and let old hurts affect you unduly, one thing you CAN take from the past is a look at those situations where you felt comfortable and confident about how you looked and compare them to the times when your confidence was pretty shaky.

Are there things that you can learn from the time you felt good about your appearance? For example:

- I was appropriately dressed.

- I knew where I was going because I looked up the route in advance and I left enough time to get there so I was calm and collected.

- I took the time to wear light makeup and apply it well.

- I'd been to the hairdressers so my hair was neat.

- I had a good-sized bag with me that meant I didn't have loads of different things to carry and my hands were free.

- I was able to forget about how I looked for the most part and focus on other people.

These are the things you can decide to repeat any or every day if you want to feel confident about how you look.

And there may also be things you can learn from the times when you hated how you looked and it reduced your confidence. For example:

- I bumped into my ex when I was wearing my baggiest sweats with an ice cream stain on the front.

- I was nervous so I had damp patches under my arms and that made me even more anxious.

- Everyone was in formal cocktail dresses and I wore an ordinary summer dress.

- I didn't have time to wash my hair or put on makeup.

- My shoes were covered in mud and scuffed.

- My dress was too short and kept riding up and I had to keep pulling the hem down.

You know from this not to make those same mistakes again, so you never go out in baggy stained clothing, you wear a good antiperspirant, check what the dress code is for a formal occasion and so on.

If you know from the past that you find particular occasions challenging, as far as feeling confident in your looks goes, then work out some strategies in advance so that you can feel your best.

For example, if you find it difficult to feel comfortable wearing a swimsuit on the beach, potential strategies might be

- buying the best swimsuit you can afford

- making sure it is the best shape for you

- wearing a sexy cover-up to move around the beach

122

- making sure your skin is looking good and you have followed a good grooming regime to remove unwanted hair

- wearing a glamorous sun hat and sunglasses.

You might also decide to get active by swimming or playing beach volleyball as soon as you arrive so that you relax about how you look and just enjoy yourself.

The more of these types of lessons you learn from your past, the more confidence you can build.

45

Be Realistic

Many books about confidence will tell you to act as if you are confident. That works well to dupe other people, and sometimes it can help you to feel more sure of yourself if others can't see how nervous and unsure you are. But for a long-term solution, you can't dupe yourself. To be truly confident, you need to love and accept yourself exactly as you are.

There's no point in going around with the idea in your head that you are a beauty queen or supermodel (unless you are). It's important to have a realistic image of yourself and still feel good about your looks. If your parents always told you that you were the most beautiful girl in the world, it comes as a shocking blow when you come fifth in the local beauty pageant or you don't get asked out by the captain of the football team. Too much flattery is almost as bad as too little.

A healthy self-image free of distortions is what you need to accept yourself and appreciate your differences from and similarities to others.

Although there will always be someone who is more beautiful than you in the eyes of the world as a whole, you are truly beautiful in your own unique way. You need to appreciate you exactly as you are and not measure yourself against some impossible standard or anyone else.

You are used to seeing real women's faces day in, day out, and you know they don't look like pictures on a magazine cover, but it's not always the case when it comes to bodies. It's rare for us to see what real women look like, so much so that you may think your body is abnormal and everyone else is just fine.

But there is so much variation when it comes to bodies that you can pretty much guarantee that plenty of other women have a body similar to yours, though never exactly the same.

Few of us look like pin-up girls and movie stars. If you are not used to seeing real women's bodies naked (and it is likely that you are not unless you are in the medical profession), then look out for those websites that make a point of helping us see how real women look. You will find examples of these in the "Helpful Books and Websites" section at the back of the book.

46

Let Go

You probably have an image in your head of an ideal look that you think is beautiful. This may be a perfect version of you - the vision of who you think you could be if you tried hard enough. Or it may be the face and figure of someone you admire or envy. Or it may even be an amalgamation of all the messages you've picked up since you were a child about what it means to be pretty or to look beautiful.

This is the impossible standard you are measuring the real living, breathing you against.

It's time to let this image go because it's a figment of your imagination. It's just not true that there is any "must have" look for beauty, and any fake idea of perfection that you have is not helping your confidence.

Having such an image in your head does not even serve you well as a goal, something to strive for. That's because it narrows your options and keeps you confined in a little bubble of what being perfect or beautiful means. In any case, true beauty in a woman is not just a look. It's a combination of many things that make up her whole being.

47

Know What Matters

Although this book is all about feeling more confident about how you look, your self-esteem should never be based on looks alone. In fact, don't base your worth on anything external such as prestige, popularity, wealth, power, connections, or possessions. It's all about who you are as a person with your particular values and qualities.

If you think you're special because of how you look, your confidence can easily crumble. One bad haircut or one rejection from a hot date and "poof" - the whole basis of your confidence and self-esteem has gone up in blue smoke.

In any case, who wants to be some plastic Barbie-doll-like perfect woman? No doubt you would be the envy of women around you and hot enough to attract men at the bar, but perfect looks won't help with keeping friends or make the one man you care about love you to bits for a lifetime. That has very little to do with hotness of looks and everything to do with hotness of character and personality - the inner qualities we are talking about.

Base your self-worth on anything less than who you are as a person and you are in danger of thinking too little or too much of yourself and taking yourself too seriously.

If you feel good because of your wealth, class or good looks, for example, then you may be tempted to look down on others, and that will be obvious in your attitude - making you less attractive than you otherwise would be.

If you feel inferior because of those external qualities, it will be obvious in your attitude that you don't think much of yourself, and therefore why should anyone else value you?

Feeling good about yourself as a person, on the other hand, makes you seem genuine, open and friendly, and that is highly attractive to everyone else. You have a genuine glow which can't be found in a beauty salon.

130

So get comfortable with how you look but don't get smug. As in all things, there is a balance. If you think you are focused too much on your appearance, set a timer for ten minutes and write a description of yourself as a whole person.

Begin as soon as the timer starts with whatever comes to mind, and don't stop writing until the timer goes off. Write everything you can about you, what you do, what you value and believe in, the character traits you have, your personality, how you contribute to the world around you, and what you are proud of. You will be pleasantly surprised when you read your description back by how much there is to you beyond your appearance.

48

Create Another Definition
Of Beauty

When you take a bit of time to think about it, beauty is so much more than a pretty face and figure. If you consider the women you most admire and think of as beautiful, there is almost certainly more to them than you see on the surface.

The women you find beautiful will not be perfect (because no one is), but they will have a certain something about them that you admire, even if you have only been aware of their physical image so far. Your real definition of beauty could probably be extended to incorporate some of these things:

- kindness

- poise

- grace

- charm

- positive attitude

- confidence

- charisma

- unique style

- compassion

- cheerfulness

- self-awareness

- empathy

- understanding

- intelligence

Every beauty icon who ever lived has possessed many of these traits, not just physical good looks. In fact, it's difficult to be a beauty if you are the very opposite of all of these things - the spiteful bitch with neither grace nor charm is never beautiful no matter how regular her features or slim her waist.

What does this mean for you?

Recognize what beauty really is and claim those traits that you already have. Put them on your list of what is good about you that you created in Strategy 4, or add them to your description from Strategy 47. Celebrate the fact that there are even more aspects to you than you thought that are truly beautiful. Then take on board those things that you would like to aspire to and work on them so that you can claim them for yourself.

49

Notice Diversity

Sometimes we get caught up in our own narrow world, with our prejudices and judgments about what is good or bad, beautiful or undesirable, and we rarely think beyond that or question it. But there is a whole world of beauty out there.

Whenever you travel, watch a foreign movie or go to a place which has a good cultural mix, notice the different forms that beauty takes, ones that are different to traditional standards of beauty in your culture. This will help you understand more than ever that beauty is not one look that you have to conform to but many different looks and styles that women have.

The factors common to beautiful women are never color of skin, eyes and hair. They are not perfect makeup or bodies. They are not particular ways of dressing or one age or another. Beauty is in the whole aura a woman projects. It is more about those things you thought about in Strategy 48 than a particular look.

If nothing else, this little exercise should help you understand that perfection in beauty is a myth, and that your look can be perfect for you, even if it does not conform to the narrow definition you used to have of beauty.

50

Remind Yourself You Can Feel Better Than You Do Now

If you are feeling a bit low and lacking in confidence at the moment, but you don't always feel like that, remind yourself of how you can feel better about how you look without too much time or effort so that you know you don't have to feel like this forever. Your reminders might take the form of

- I love my hair when I have just washed and dried it.

- I feel beautiful when I am ready for a night out.

- I feel good when I am wearing smart clothes for work.

- My sea-green dress looks great with my skin and hair color.

- My hair looks good when I wear it up.

- I look prettier when I take five minutes to put on some makeup.

- I'll feel better once I'm showered and dressed.

- I love it when my nails are manicured and I'm wearing nail polish that goes with my outfit.

- A trip to the hairdressers for a cut and color will do me good.

Then go and do one or more of the things on your reminder list until you feel better about your looks. Once you have done this exercise once, keep your list and continually add items to it when you think of them, so you have a ready-made list of things to do that boost your confidence.

These reminders will help you realize you can look better any time you like, and that's a good thing for your state of mind.

But you can also give yourself a boost by reminding yourself how much you are loved exactly as you look now. Just think of all those people in your life who would be happy to give you a hug when you are down, no matter how you look. Create another list of them and call one up or ask for a hug.

51

Get Your Body Worries In Perspective

Your worries about how you look may seem overwhelming at times. You can fixate on the size of your nose, your flat chest or your wobbly thighs. But in the vast scheme of things, how important are they? Sometimes you just need to get a sense of the wonder of everything and where you fit in to feel at peace with yourself.

When you get the chance, go somewhere that lets you see the magnificence and sheer scale of the natural world. This might be sitting on the sand by the ocean with the waves crashing on the shore, a walk in a mountain range or just a marvelous view across a valley. If all else fails, gaze at the stars in the sky on a clear night. And then think about how insignificant your nose or your thighs or whatever really are compared to everything else in nature, and how you have a life to live in the vast universe that is out there. Don't waste it worrying about your nose.

52

Focus On Other People

If you feel self-conscious and worried about how you look, get out of your own head and focus your thoughts on other people.

In a crowd, you can do this simply by people watching. If you are in a conversation, try to listen intently to what is being said.

Don't just look at and listen to the obvious, look for the expressions on faces and body language to understand what is really going on with others. Once you become engrossed in working out their thoughts and feelings, you will be less wrapped up in your own worries.

This is a great strategy to make you feel less worried about yourself. Understanding what makes people tick, being present (instead of in your own head) when you are in the company of others, and deeply listening to whoever is talking will make you a better friend, even a better human being and that will give you good feelings about yourself too.

53

Expand Your Confidence

Everything you do to feel more confident about yourself in general helps you feel more confident about how you look. When you feel good as a whole person, you can't help but like yourself more and feel good about your body that is really just the container for all that you are.

So don't stop at only improving your confidence in how you look, work on it in every way you can.

Here are some examples of things you can do to improve your general confidence:

- Have a list of things you would like to accomplish over the next year or so. Include easy fun activities you haven't tried before, places you would like to visit as well as more serious things you want to do. Setting goals and ticking them off is a great way to feel good about yourself and broaden your experience so that you feel confident about doing more things.

- Take problems in your stride. Confident people are positive and optimistic. Remember you and your life have a mass of possibilities that are there for the taking. Every experience is valuable. Look at setbacks and problems as things you can learn from and use to move forward, not as the end of the world.

- Make the things you are passionate about a priority. Show yourself that what you care about is important enough to you to make time for. It's not something to be squashed in favor of what others want you to do.

- Be friendly and open with those you meet. Have a smile and a few words for everyone and look them in the eye when you speak to them. You will have more success relating to people and feel better about yourself as a result.

If you would like more ideas for how to expand your general confidence, pick up the free bonus that comes with this book

"Rock-solid Confidence Step By Step: How To Be Confident And Happy With Yourself." Details are in the "FREE for you" section below (page 152). You will feel so much better about every part of your life.

FINALLY

Congratulations! You've arrived at the final part of this book. You now have 53 strategies to choose from to be more confident and happier with yourself. If you put some of these techniques into practice, you can't help but feel good. Now it's time to choose where you want to start and begin your campaign.

Sometimes the road to confidence is a rocky one, but by taking one step at a time, you will get there. In any case, you'll always be streets ahead of where you would be if you hadn't even started. So don't wait for the perfect time to feel good about yourself. The perfect time is now.

Once you've read to the very end, loop right around to the start of the book and decide on a plan of action. Two or three strategies is a great start.

What's Next? More Confidence?

This book covered just one aspect of what I call "Captivating Confidence" – feeling SO good about yourself that you can't fail to have more success out there in the world and attract others to you.

"You Are Beautiful! 53 Easy Ways To Love Your Imperfect Self" is actually part of a series of guides that help you have

148

more confidence in life, particularly the kind of confidence you need to be happy in love.

When it comes to dating and relationships, confidence is essential. Without a good dose of it, you'll find it difficult to

- enjoy happy long-term relationships as an equal to your partner

- get to know guys you like

- have them recognize you as "the one"

- hold your own when it comes to calling the shots

- move on from guys who don't treat you right

- trust a guy enough to open up so he gets to know you and love you on the deepest level.

The "Captivating Confidence" guides help you have all the confidence you need to create rock-solid relationships whether it's getting to know guys and feeling more confident flirting with them or feeling better about yourself after a breakup so that you're ready to find a new love. There's also help with the confidence you need to enjoy first dates, find love via online dating or keep the spark going in a long-term relationship.

Next In The Series: How To Feel Good Naked

With the first "Captivating Confidence" guide "You Are Beautiful! 53 Easy Ways To Love Your Imperfect Self," you discovered a series of strategies to help you feel good about yourself wherever you are, whether you are at home doing chores or out at a party, and many of those strategies are equally useful when you want to feel confident about how you look in bed with a partner.

But because stripping off in front of a lover, especially a new one, can make even the most confident of us feel vulnerable, there are a number of special strategies you can use to feel great when it's time to reveal all. By working on your confidence specifically for those times, you will find it easier to relax and enjoy yourself.

With the second in the "Captivating Confidence" series, you'll find a further 35 strategies to feel happy about yourself and your body no matter what state of undress you're in with a guy. If that kind of confidence is something that you would like to develop, keep an eye out for this book. You will be amazed at how delighted you can feel even naked in company!

You can get news of all the new releases in the "Captivating Confidence" series including "Feel Good Naked: 35 Secrets Of Irresistible Body Confidence" when you get your FREE book (see next page).

More Confidence: $9.99
or FREE For You

If you would like to have more self-confidence in every area of your life, pick up a copy of the companion book in this series "Rock-solid Confidence Step By Step: How To Be Confident And Happy With Yourself" It's available in paperback priced at $9.99.

Alternatively, you can download it absolutely FREE with my best wishes, as a thank you for your interest in this book, in exchange for answering one quick question about confidence. Get all the details here:

http://lovefromana.com/moreconfidence

As well as the book, you'll get the latest news and updates from the author including future free reports and useful guides.

Helpful Books And Websites

realwomensbodies.com

This website explores the whole topic of body image and has the goal of helping to build a healthy positive image of real women in the world at large and in our own minds.

"Hopefully this site will leave you feeling better about your own body as you begin to see the true beautiful variety of real women's bodies."

007b.com

A whole website on loving your breasts just as they are - big, small, pert, sagging, uneven, flat. If you have particular problems accepting this part of your body, take a look. There are hundreds of pictures in galleries of real women's breasts,

154

and after a few minutes browsing there, you will realize that yours are perfect just the way they are, whatever their size and shape.

abeautifulbodyproject.com

Well worth a look, the Beautiful Body Project is about acceptance of the beauty of the whole female body in all its forms. It is a platform and network of female photographers dedicated to creating therapeutic and truthful photos, videos and stories to help women and girls build self-esteem.

theshapeofamother.com

This site provides a look at the real bodies of women who have been pregnant. This is a good site for support if you were happy with your body before you had a child and are less happy with it now. Shape Of A Mother is "where we share photos of our bodies before, during and after pregnancy to know we are not alone in the changes that happen to us."

Dove Videos

Whatever you think about a beauty company trying to promote a healthy body image while still trying to sell products, you have to admire this one for at least recognizing the issue. With their "Campaign for Real Beauty," Dove are trying to get women to recognize that beauty comes in many forms - ones that you don't usually find in advertising. And given that their products are simple beauty basics and not the priciest, it's not as if they are pushing products that women don't want or need.

You'll find some great videos on youtube.com. Look for (without quotes) "dove evolution," "dove body evolution," "dove amy" and "dove onslaught." These videos are designed to make you think – and they do.

Other Books From The Publisher

Ten Years Younger In A Weekend

Forget Botox, cosmetic surgery, expensive skin creams you can't afford, and punishing regimens. This is a collection of all the things you can do to look good at any age, right now. See *beautytoptotoe.com/ten-years-younger* for details.

Fitness In No Time

For those who don't have much time but want to be fit and healthy, here is a simple program for beginners you can do in ten minutes three times a week to get fit, strong and supple.

Every body deserves 30 minutes a week. For details see *simplyfitnessgear.com/notime/*

Walk Your Way To Weight Loss With Your Pedometer

A program which is as much about getting healthy as it is about losing excess pounds. See *walkoffweight.org* for details.

Excite Diet: Beat Diet Boredom

If you're bored with the same old diets, this book can help motivate you to keep going as you get to choose a new strategy every day and vary them as much as you like to fit in with your lifestyle and plans. See *excitedietbook.com* for all 50 ways to beat diet boredom.

THANK YOU!

I hope you enjoyed this, the first book in the "Captivating Confidence" series. You're now armed with the strategies you need to feel not just great but fantastic about your own unique look.

If you like the book, I'd appreciate it if you could leave a short review where you made your purchase. It will help me improve this and future books and help other women decide if "You Are Beautiful! 53 Easy Ways To Love Your Imperfect Self" is right for them too.

Let's spread the message far and wide that real women are beautiful just as they are.

About the Author

Like many women these days, Ana Wilde is a full-time juggler of multiple roles. She is a writer, researcher and publisher, owner of a small business. She lives with her husband and two kids in an old house in Scotland, where she is chief cook and bottle washer as well as finder of all lost things. Find Ana online at *LoveFromAna.com*.

Other Books By Ana

182 Great Places to Meet Men: Get The Guy You Want

PLAY! 77 Sexy Games For Two To Spice Up Your Love Life

In The Captivating Confidence Series

Feel Good Naked: 35 Secrets Of Irresistible Body Confidence

Contact The Author

Feedback, questions and comments are welcome via email. I'd love to hear from you. You can get in touch with me at any time via my email address ana@lovefromana.com.

Love from

Ana

P.S. You're welcome to join in the fun by commenting and sharing here too:

Blog: http://lovefromana.com

Twitter: https://twitter.com/lvfromana

Facebook: https://www.facebook.com/lovefromana

Join The Love From Ana Reader Panel

If you liked this book and want to be part of the reader panel who review pre-release copies of future books, please send me an email at ana@lovefromana.com mentioning you would like to take part and I will be in touch.

160

Made in the USA
Middletown, DE
13 July 2016